NEVER HELD A GUN

Guy James Whitworth

rainshadow

ISBN: (paperback) 978-0-6486361-1-3
ISBN: (hardcover) 978-0-6486361-2-0

www.guyjameswhitworth.com

Published by rainshadow, an imprint of Clouds of Magellan Press, Melbourne

www.cloudsofmagellanpress.net

Cover and artwork by Guy James Whitworth

Design by G Thompson

Contents

The important thing about relationships

A man that's never held a gun

I'm not saying that it's wrong to stand your ground and fight.
Stand tall, stand proud, stand for what is right.
Let's change the fucking world, but let's do it our way.
Make our voices heard, still let others have their say.
I want to bring about change, I want to get things done.
But I want to be a man that's never held a gun.

I refuse to use fear, for my own means and end,
Or abuse what I hold dear, play masculine pretend.
I want the peace that's in me, to mend the pieces of you,
I'll use compassion, kindness and love as the glue.
A philosophy that's brave, though some will turn and run,
But I want to be a man that's never held a gun.

Let's not weaponise our differences, trade blow for blow.
Turn the other cheek, we are more alike than we know.
I don't want to win a race, because the other runner falls.
We need to make wider tables, not build higher walls.
No one truly wins when a war is won,
And I want to be a man that's never held a gun.

Kaleidoscope dream

Today I saw the most wonderful blue,
No word of a lie, perfectly true.
Recalling that memory, so heavy in bed,
I also remember a sumptuous red.
Then recollect other colours I've seen –
Berry-like purples, deep forest green.
I'm feeling so sleepy, yet it's hard not to think
Luxurious turquoise, loud shocking pink!
A bright kaleidoscope morphs to a dream,
Swirling gold, indigo, fuchsia and cream.
These colours so vivid, so rich, and so real,
Yellow, sapphire, orange, and teal.
Every shade and colour, from dark through to bright.
As this rainbow surrounds me, I bid you good night.

⇌ Something on your mind

Waiting

A letter to my younger self

They flew by so quickly, those years in my prime,
So I'm writing this letter, to send back in time.
To a much younger me, who has time left to spare,
With a waistline, optimism, ambition, and hair.

They're gonna be messy these many years ahead,
Jeez, there's gonna be times you'll wish yourself dead.
Such as, after a breakup, when you turn twenty-five,
Search for joy in the little things, that'll keep you alive.

In your thirties you'll realise all you could be,
You knew of this earlier but chose not to see.
When you finally let people in, the more you'll belong,
Embrace so-called weaknesses, they're what'll make you
strong.

It really does get better, hell, it even gets fun,
Try to learn from the moments it all comes undone.
Don't confuse happiness for the trappings of wealth,
Do invest widely, in the prospect of health.

Never wear outfits with horizontal stripes,
And never feel guilty for late boozy nights.
Get yourself a therapist, it's really for the best,
You'll be far happier when some issues are addressed.

Don't be afraid to use the word NO,
Certain friends that you lose, it's a blessing they go.
Avoid arseholes called Adam, Darren and Bob,
Don't trade your ethics for the sake of a job.

Do trust in the process, all wounds heal in time,
Spoiler alert, you're going to be fine.
Lastly forgive yourself for bad choices in men,
When you've become me, you'll want to do it all again.

The bravest thing a man can do

Check your dominance, I like to say to men,
Or live through the consequences, again and again.
The bravest thing a man can do is learn to be humble,
Ask for help, apologise, admit it when you stumble.
Toxicity is made from a compounding fear
Of appearing to be weak, when really it's clear:
Regardless of gender we're all fragile beings.
Extreme masculinity is nothing worth seeing.
It builds walls, where we should be sowing seeds,
Sabotages growth and blocks out needs.
So, live through the consequences, again and again,
Or check your dominance, as I like to say to men.

⇆ Heavy Lifting

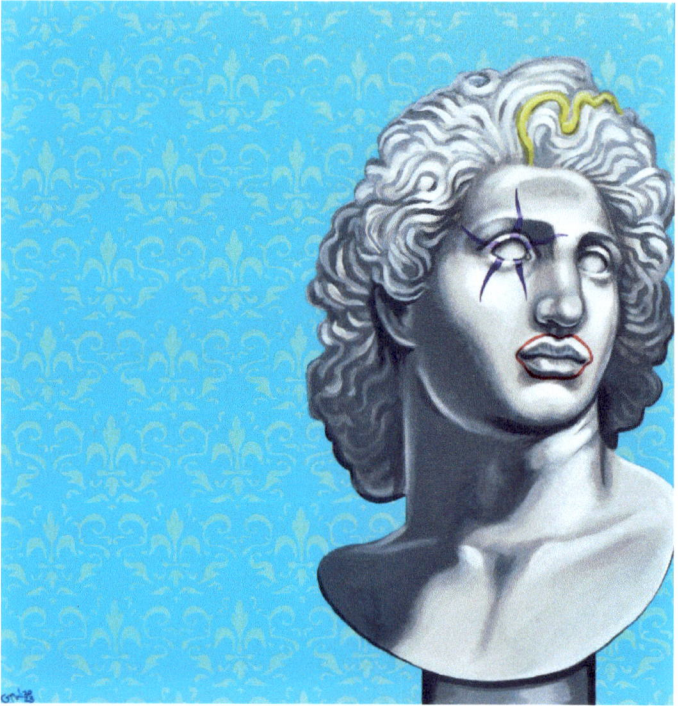

If you've got something to say

One more for the road

Let's get munted; a bottle of gin and a joint.
We could face the world sober; but really, what's the point?
Society is crumbing we're all running out of time.
There's a chance it might look prettier through a glass of wine.

I've found if I'm clear-headed it all looks pretty grim,
There are no nobler last words than 'fill it to the brim'.
If we can't dance while the world burns what else can we do?
I reckon molly and martinis might just get us through.

And if there's no tomorrow then hangovers aren't a fear.
If whisky makes you frisky maybe it's time you had a beer.
Raise a glass to what could have been as we watch it all implode,
No one is going anywhere, so let's have one more for the road.

Ooh, ain't she butch

Fuzzy wuzzy Velcro

Who doesn't love a bear with a round furry bum.
Who wouldn't want a cuddle, a tickle, and some fun.
Within big solid arms and weathered salty skin,
Strong legs, broad shoulders, and a wide knowing grin.

I lust after cheeky winks, not an hourglass waist.
Those smooth twinky-dinks, they just aren't to my taste,
But to feast on what's found in that wilderness of fur,
When it comes to chunky monkeys, I'm quite the connoisseur.

Toned, tight and shiny, I'd happily trade them in,
For the fuzzy wuzzy Velcro between pubes and chin.
What tickles my pickle is to tug on the rug,
Whilst that weight's upon my face in a loving bear-hug.

Queer iconography

My Own Trophy Room

If I had a medal pinned on me every time I tried,
A plaque commemorating every tear I cried.
Presented with a certificate every point I failed,
Or a ticker tape parade for every plan derailed.
A shiny gold statuette, for every 'no' acquired,
Attended glamorous ceremonies when a plan backfired.
Honoured with accolades if a door slammed in my face,
A celebratory handshake for not finishing the race.
Knighted for disappointments by men with shiny swords,
If we celebrated failure, where would I keep all my awards?

Golden moment

This is the big one

This is the big one, from which neither will recover,
Scars on our hearts in the shape of each other.
I've dreaded this ending even before we began,
Multitudes of miseries made missing one man.

The rest of forever to regret these mistakes,
The more that we loved, the more it now aches.
Onwards and upwards, let's pretend we may heal,
Though never quite mending this pain that I feel.

I can pull down the shutters put barriers in place,
Do everything I can not to picture your face.
Every cliché, every instant, every action is pain,
From these moments on life will never be the same.

Seven for a secret

There is a time

After the world has taken
All that it can take
There is a time – it's wisest –
To let yourself break
To let it all fracture
Shatter apart
See it not as a measure
Or mark of your heart

Yield to the tension
No need to be strong
After keeping it together
For so very long
There's a time to carry it
All on your back
And a time to let it
Tumble crumble and crack

In a world full of burdens
When you've had your fill
Simply let it all
Fall wherever it will
Take on nothing more
For your own sake
There is a time – it's wisest
To let yourself break

Hear no evil

Let's get through this together

Nothing makes a difference, and nothing is forever
I don't have the answers, let's get through this together

From the baby dykes in glitter to the daddy in his pleather
Just dance with me and know, we can get through this together

Whether you're an old friend, or a new one, any way, whatever
If our eyes met even briefly, let's get through this together

Doesn't matter how you identify (queer, cis, trans, whoever)
I see you; I embrace you: we can get through this together

Let's all take this feeling and make it last forever
All of us are different, but let's get through this together

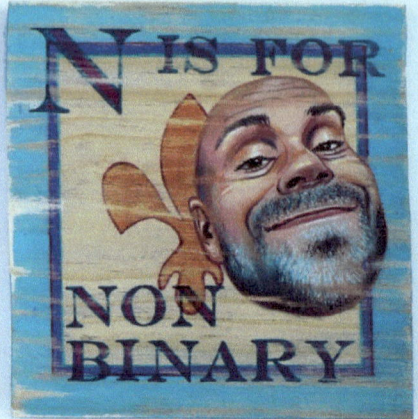

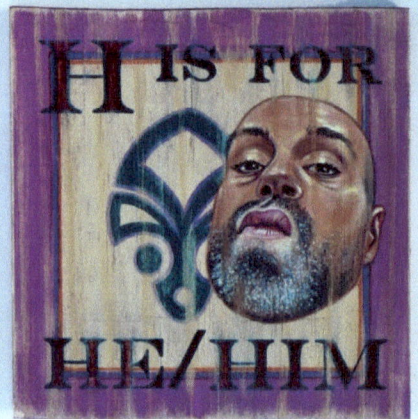

Personal politics

A counterclockwise life

Gender is a construct
I never bought into that deal
Think it's pretty fucked
That you'd tell me how to feel.
No option but to fight
To swim against the tide
And hold on extra tight
On this rollercoaster ride
Not happy as a boy
Not feeling like a girl
Still entitled to feel joy
In this counterclockwise world

Classical Queerdom

Thank you for bearing witness

Thank you for bearing witness to all that I have been
Thank you for being present, through the dramas and routine
When other friends were absent you were there to share the pain
Helped me bear the burden, knew when to take the reins

It was easy to keep going, knowing you'd be there to break my fall
When I stumbled, when I messed up, and lost my bearing on it all
I certainly wasn't perfect and made mistakes along the way
But I knew you'd never judge me, abandon, or betray

You've supported and encouraged me in all that I have done
Held my hand when it was darkest, opened curtains to the sun
Through glories and disappointments,
                              throughout everything we've seen
I thank you for bearing witness to all that I have been

There's a constant disappointment …

There's a constant disappointment
that follows me around,
The tiniest of distractions
like some distant ringing sound.
Never in my line of sight –
yet never far away,
Certainly not strong enough
to trigger total disarray.
Like a memory of a dream
forgotten long ago;
A seed awaiting germination,
sensing circumstance to grow.
Yet it colours every action
each decision that I make,
Subtly and rhythmically,
quite impossible to shake.
As reliable as clockwork
as solid as the ground,
There's a constant disappointment
that follows me around.

⇐ Golden rays 2

I love you

Whatsitgonnabe?

That long hard stare is menacing,
but also, kinda hot.
How do I know if you're up for it –
or if you're really not?
Tingly thrills not knowing
what's going to happen next.
You gonna holler for a policeman?
Or invite me home for sex?

Pound my hole or punch my face?
It could go either way.
So hard to tell anymore
who's straight, bi, pan or gay.
You gonna rough me up, or push me down?
I can't wait to see.
Beat me up or beat me off,
oooh, whatsitgonnabe?

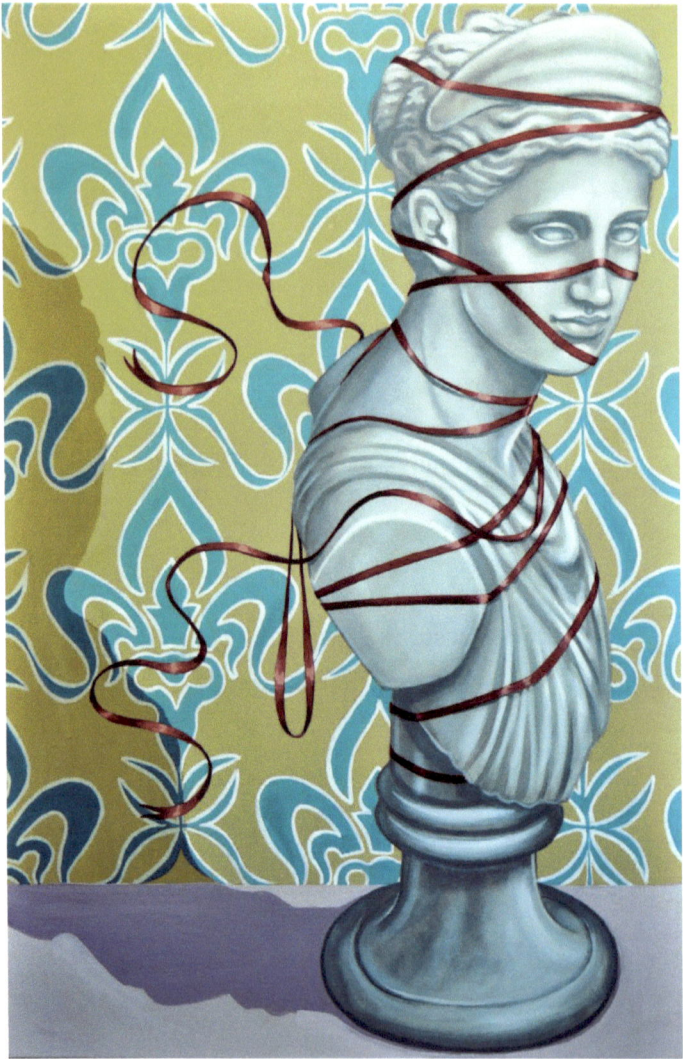

A little tied up here

News from a far-off familiar land

News from a far-off familiar land,
Provokes an emotion I struggle to understand.
Decades forgotten yet eternally the same,
Heartache reignites at the sound of your name.
Red buses, nostalgia, antiquity and beer,
Early learnings of what it meant to be queer.

Hedonistic times and the folly of youth
Discovering ourselves and denying the truth.
Knowing the streets we walked down so well,
The sound of you laughing and Cockney Bow Bells.
Charing Cross Road on the coldest of nights,
Vinegar-soaked chips and Piccadilly lights.

Summer in Clapham and Lavender Hill.
Are there people just like us living there still?
Running through Kings Cross to avoid being bashed.
Falling asleep on the last train, so trashed.
Duckie, the Fridge and Substation South,
Dancing and tasting the drink in your mouth.

Dreaming of who we knew we'd become,
Biking through Battersea, chasing the sun.
Joyous frivolity in a dark, rainy place.
I can't help but smile at the thought of your face.
You'll always be dreaming and dancing through time.
The news is you've gone, and the memory just mine.

Shine

What it means to be a man

I've never been a fan
Of what it means to be a man.
I don't wish to dish the dirt,
but masculinity just doesn't work.

For me.

The finery of your binary ideal
Just doesn't appeal.
Like black and white
and day and night.

I've always much preferred
The subtle blues and pinks that dusk confers.
Glorious in-betweens
And all that means.

Unpicking binary at the seams.

My Queerdom is mine
Not yours to define.
Like gender I can render
where on that scale I am.
Only I decide
on life's bumpy ride
What it means to be this man.

Blind like love and justice

Married men are fun

There's a pale band on your finger where a wedding ring should be
When you tell your wife about this trip, I doubt you'll mention me.
The fanciest of restaurants, yet we're tucked in the back room
When we sign into the hotel, what will be your *nom de plume*?

I smell bullshit in the tales you tell, your stuffy closet stinks.
But I'll keep laughing at your jokes, if you keep buying drinks.
Nothing about you interests me more than the cash you spend.
I'm not hoping that we stay in touch – I'm not looking for a friend.

So, you were pressured into marriage, and all that society dictates.
I don't doubt you're homophobic with your family and your mates.
The way you choose to live your life is completely up to you,
I just hope your wife is happy and takes secret lovers too.

Married men are fun, a lucrative wine-dine sixty-nine.
When we wake shame-faced tomorrow none of the guilt is mine.
I only hope if you have queer kids, you allow them to be free,
So your sons won't hide in backrooms telling lies to men like me.

What do I mean?

Remember when

When you're questioning the testing of how much you can endure
Remember dosage is the difference between a poison and a cure.

When everyone wants too much and the demands are way too high
Remember some people never fail, because some people never try.

When disaster and disappointment seem intensely intertwined
Remember these lessons are your blessings, so smile, and just be kind.

Lifetimes of listening (straya my home)

Out in the open lorikeets squawk overhead,
Earth underneath me, ancient, iron rich red.
Sun this strong was never meant for freckled skin,
To tame nature through force is a battle we can't win.
You bore a crown and rifle to hammer at this door,
And your descendants can't deny that fact anymore.

Sounds of waves crashing, gum trees reach up high,
The horizon a straight line, equal half sea and sky.
White tears on red earth won't break any drought.
Sorry doesn't cut it, when it's used as a way out
Of difficult conversations, around ownership of land,
Apologies mean nothing, with a weapon in your hand.

Paperbark, wattle-brush, mountains of blue,
We were never invited; the rent is long overdue.
White guilt and shame, form denial and spite,
Too much for a single generation to ever put right.
A reverberating cry cuts across land, sea and air,
It will take lifetimes of listening and work to repair.

Straya, Straya, as troubled as it's wide.
Both heaven or hell, two worlds side by side.
Honesty that's painful, changing the systems we are in
Are the only ways forward, the only ways to begin.
After the oldest of cultures met the greediest of men,
Can this country ever be unified again?

⇐ Ned

43

Elegant chaos

If only I were free

Oh, the places I would go to,
The things that I would see,
If only I were able,
If only I were free.
The lovers that would love me,
The chances I would take,
If only I was open
And allowed myself to wake.
To the wonders that await me,
And the struggles I would win,
Oh, if only I could muster,
And let my life begin.

Yet these walls I've built around me
Are as tall as they are wide.
Bricks of apathy and idleness
Keep me anxiously inside.
Gaps in cages I've constructed
Still temptingly reveal
That excitement still awaits me
With a hint of what I'd feel.

Achieving wants and aspirations
Are my own lessons to teach.
Once I pick myself up
There'll be no height I cannot reach.
Oh yes, the places I would go to
The things that I would see,
If only I were able,
If only I were free.

I'm the richest man that ever set foot upon this earth

Some want to bathe in diamonds, I get to bathe in love.
Good fortune showers down on me, like rain from up above.
Without doubt, I am the richest man you will ever meet.
Although not in pounds or dollars traded on Wall Street.

What I've earnt and what I appreciate are two very different things,
The achievements of these hands is never wearing fancy rings.
I could walk the length of my possessions, if laid out side by side,
In only just a few steps, and I have no treasures I need to hide.

Everything of value, and everything I own,
Was gifted to me by others, or lovingly through loan.
My workpants may be threadbare and my jacket roughly patched,
Yet I've an opulence of riches that really can't be matched.

My head is never heavy from a jewel encrusted crown,
Nothing bearing a sovereign's head weighs my pockets down.
Proudly my heart is buoyant and gets to soar care-free,
Ornamented only by my memories of those who value me.

Sunny skies, good humour, and favourable health,
And those I keep around me, they make up all my wealth.
There's nothing in my cupboards that has much monetary worth,
Still, I'm the richest man that ever set foot upon this earth.

↜ The bravery of taking flight

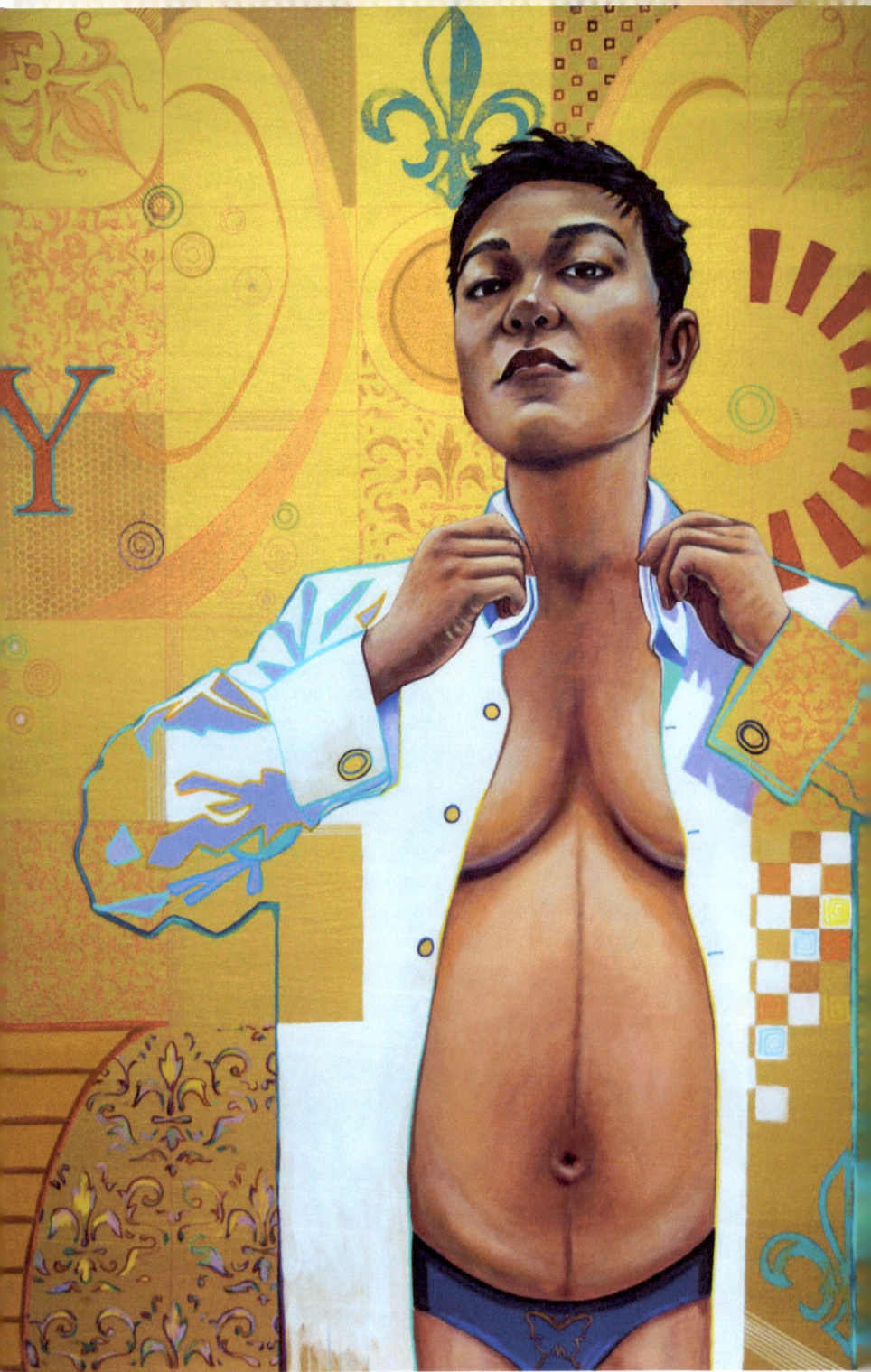

Potential fire hazard

There used to be a flame
At the sound of your name
That ignited in my heart

It used to cause a feeling
That always left me reeling
In no small part

But now I'm left dejected
Undervalued and rejected
There's barely cinders in the air

That flame of love is just a flicker
It doesn't shine or even glitter
Do you even care?

For that love to reignite
and re-illuminate the night
There's work that must be done

Stoke the flame and never smother
The potential of each other
To blaze as brightly as the sun

⇆ They/Them

Ribbons for Pell

Feel free to believe what you want to believe

Feel free to believe what you want to believe,
Such as your celestial saviour was never conceived,
But was his own father, via virgin birth,
Dead for 3 days, but then came back to earth.
And when Eve bit into the apple, she created sin,
However, we're all born of sinners, so none of us can win.

Yet if you eat of his flesh, and drink of his blood,
He'll absolve you of sin and won't drown us in a flood.
Just remember, when your sky Lord tells you what to do,
No one else is bound to that, it's really only you.
See, I don't believe in your version of Christ,
I think it's just the truth that you've sacrificed.

To me, religious teaching seems designed to oppress
The masses, and keep them suffering, under duress.
You claim that you are love, yet seem driven by hate,
With the capacity to justify that at some mythical gate.
I like to keep it simple, my beliefs aren't that complex,
I'll just keep it real in this life, not worry about the next.

When will be the last time?

When will be the last time
My name is ever said?
And when will be the last time
This book is ever read?

When will be the last time
I hurry to catch a train?
And when will be the last time
We run together through the rain?

When will be the last time
We see the inside of this place?
And when will be the last time
I kiss your silly face?

When will be the last time
You ever make me cry?
And when will be the last time
We realise time has passed us by?

⇐ My time to go

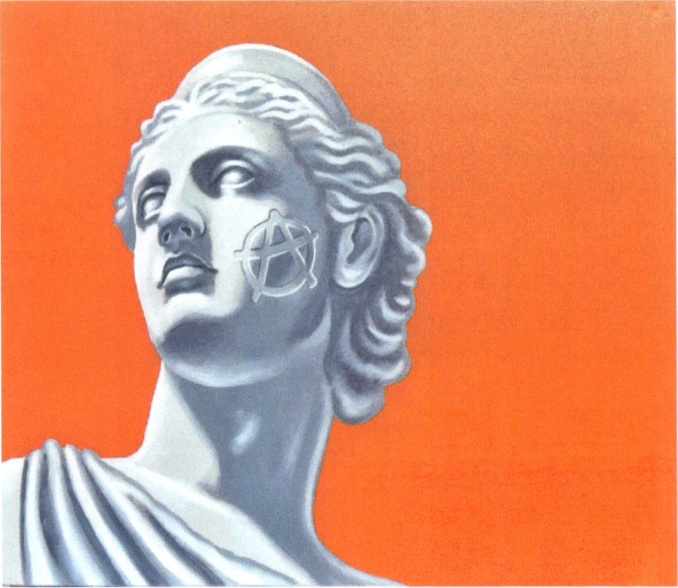

A is for

My masterpiece

Maybe my masterpiece will not be
a particular work of art
but the creation of a person able to move through the world
without showing how damaged and defeated they really are

Queering the landscape

Pride march

Glorious acceptance
With the happiest of beats
Glitter in the air
As we take to the streets

Masculine women
Feminine men
Waves of happiness
Again and again.

Laughing with strangers
Streamers in the sky
Dancing in my lovers' arms
So safe that I could cry

Wrapped in rainbow ribbons
Rejecting monochrome
Strength in Queerdom
These communities are home

A very brief moment in time

All of this will come to pass

It's hard, I know, but it's just for now
Time moves on, though we can't predict how
Everything will evolve, change and grow
So feel the now, but also know
Whether it's heavy as hell
Or it cuts like glass
All of this will come
to pass.

What is it that you want to say?

While I hold you tight
And look you in the eye
Tell me how
Tell me who
Tell me why.

Like little birds, set the words you're thinking free,
The weight you carry, come, lay it down by me.

Whisper it through tears
Or yell it bravely to the sky
Liberate and let it leave you
Let it loose
Let it fly.

Scatter words into the wind, unlock secrets, turn the key
Take all the time you need, I've nowhere else I need to be

Leave here wlth no burden
Carry home no shame
Say a time
a place
A space and say a name.

Lay your worries down, carry them not after this day,
I'll be silent now, what is it that you want to say?

⇄ Follow the lines

Know your own worth

You are amazing
You are unique.
Quite formidable
Complete.
Destined for greatness
From the time of your birth.
Yet your potential goes unrealised
If you don't know your own worth.

You are special
You are divine.
Quite spectacular
Sublime.
You make the world a better place
With every step upon this earth.
But all of this means nothing
If you don't know your own worth.

⇇ Golden rays 1

QL299

There's a silly war a-coming

There's a silly war a-coming,
a battle between left and right.
It's not even a war worth fighting,
like the one between black and white.
It's pitting those that love nostalgia
and idealise what's been,
Against those that want to build a future
and know the past's a dream.

It's going to be silly and unnecessary,
with losses on either side,
Bloodshed and destruction,
ripping families open wide.
The only way it can be avoided is
if both sides take the time,
To realise silliness, and entitlement,
could become a war crime.

Disappearing act

Hello Mr Pigeon

Good morning Mr Pigeon
You've got a funny walk.
I wonder what's your story?
If only you could talk.

Good day to you Mr Pigeon
As you fly around the streets.
Rummaging through the rubbish
And finding all the treats.

Good afternoon Mr Pigeon
I'm so jealous you can fly.
Everywhere's your playground
With your friends up in the sky.

Good evening Mr Pigeon
But I must hurry on my way.
I hope you enjoyed your adventures
And all you saw today!

Good night Mr Pigeon
I hope your nest is warm and deep
High up on the rooftops
As you settle down to sleep.

I need you to listen

This isn't how I want us to be.
To unlock these prisons, communication is key.
Your words overwhelm me and get in my way,
'Til I can't even remember what I intended to say.
So angrily I love you – a juxtaposition –
Words choose to fail me when you choose not to listen.

We talk over each other, each of us right,
Ready to argue, eager to fight.
Pausing, exhausted, battled and weary,
I've so much to tell you if you'd bother to hear me.
This inevitable outcome is pain and collision,
In familiar terrain where you choose not to listen.

I gave you your airtime, let you speak first,
Filled with intention and resentment I'm ready to burst.
Breathless, I stumble my words tumble out,
Passion takes over, unwisely I shout.
We do this so often, it's become a tradition,
Let's do this differently, I need you to listen.

The louder I get, the more you refuse,
To consider my viewpoint and words that I use.
Your deafness defeats me, defies sense or theory,
I'm wasting my breath, if you choose not to hear me.
It shouldn't be a warzone or a bloody competition,
For the very last time, I'm asking you to listen.

⇄ Wanting

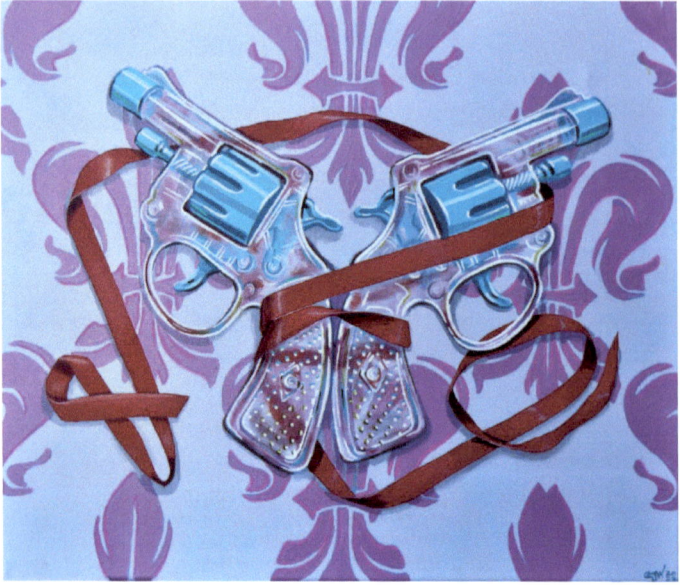

Bloodlines A

Aggressive accessories

You wear your extremisms like casual accessories,
a racist belt
A misogynistic hat
A homophobic clutch bag
A tie made from finest ableism
A scarf of hand-knitted transphobia
Worn with such attitude
like a model in a show
inspiring
loathing
wherever you go

Guy James Whitworth

Guy James Whitworth grew up in Northumberland, England and moved to Sydney over twenty years ago. He is one of those artists that try to use their powers for good and is as well-known for his activism around animal rights and social reform as he is for his vibrant annual exhibitions.

Guy is also co-founder of the global No Meat May initiative.

Guy is known mostly for an art practice that includes opulent portraiture that lends itself to elevating repressed and marginalised members of society, using the authority of visual art as a medium to do so. He actively shares these skills as the host of Sydney's Queer Sketch Club, a fortnightly gathering of creative and fabulous souls.

Guy has won various awards and has been finalist in many of Australia's art prizes.

His previous two books of art and essays, *Signs of a struggle* and *Enough of your nonsense,* are both published by Clouds of Magellan Press. This is his first book of poetry.

www.guyjameswhitworth.com

www.ingramcontent.com/pod-product-compliance
Lightning Source LLC
Chambersburg PA
CBHW041104110426
42740CB00043B/149